To:

From:

Compiled by Suzanne Linder

Designed by Michelle Chae
See page 81 for photo credits.

Copyright © 2007
Peter Pauper Press, Inc.
202 Mamaroneck Avenue
White Plains, NY 10601
All rights reserved
ISBN 978-1-59359-854-9
Printed in China
7 6 5 4 3 2 1

Visit us at www.peterpauper.com

Spit Happens!

Introduction

Never is a sense of humor more essential than in the early days of parenthood. *Spit Happens!* reminds us that we're not alone in the organized mayhem that characterizes life with baby.

Every little bundle of joy brings its own matching little bundle of challenges. In the wise words of writer Teresa Bloomingdale, "If your baby is beautiful and perfect, never cries or fusses, sleeps on schedule and burps on demand, an angel all the time, you're the grandma." Designed to make you smile, *Spit Happens!* reminds you that the best way to approach parenthood is with a good strong dose of humor. Because, after all, as has been said before, "A baby changes everything . . . except itself!"

It sometimes happens, even in the best of families, that a baby is born. This is not necessarily cause for alarm. The important thing is to keep your wits about you and borrow some money.

Elinor Goulding Smith

People who say they sleep like a baby usually don't have one.

Leo J. Burke

I always wondered
why babies
spend so much time
sucking their thumbs.
Then I tasted
"baby food."

Robert Orben

People often ask me, "What's the difference between couplehood and babyhood?" In a word? Moisture.

Paul Reiser

If you were to open up a baby's head—and I am not for a moment suggesting that you should—you would find nothing but an enormous drool gland.

Dave Barry

A baby is an angel whose wings decrease as his legs increase.

Author unknown

Even when freshly washed and relieved of all obvious confections, children tend to be sticky.

Fran Lebowitz

Children have never been very good at listening to their elders, but they have never failed to imitate them.

James Baldwin

There are no seven wonders of the world in the eyes of a child. There are seven million.

Walt Streightiff

The art of being a parent is to sleep when the baby isn't looking.

Author unknown

He followed in his father's footsteps, but his gait was somewhat erratic.

Nicolas Bentley

Making the decision to have a child—it's momentous. It is to decide forever to have your heart go walking around outside your body.

Elizabeth Stone

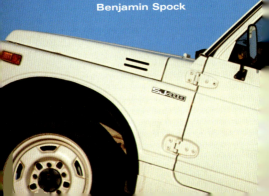

In automobile terms, the child supplies the power but the parents have to do the steering.

Benjamin Spock

> Having a family is like having a bowling alley installed in your brain.
>
> Martin Mull

A two-year-old is kind of like having a blender, but you don't have a top for it.

Jerry Seinfeld

Have children while your parents are still young enough to take care of them.

Rita Rudner

Hang around doggies and kids; they know how to play.

Geoffrey Godbey

Babies are always more trouble than you thought—and more wonderful.

Charles Osgood

I don't know why
they say
"you have a baby."
The baby has *you*.

Gallagher

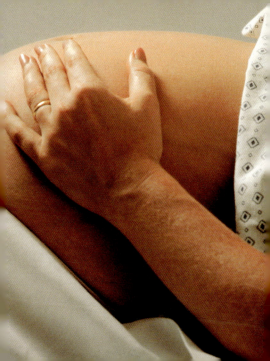

There are times when parenthood seems nothing but feeding the mouth that bites you.

Peter De Vries

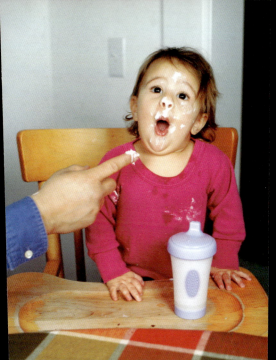

The best way to make children good is to make them happy.

Oscar Wilde

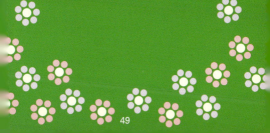

> I just can't get over
> how much babies cry.
> I really had no idea
> what I was getting into.
> To tell you the truth,
> I thought it would be more
> like getting a cat.
>
> Anne Lamott

> Every baby is a person who has language, feelings, and a unique personality—and, therefore, deserves respect.

Tracy Hogg,
The Baby Whisperer

Diaper backward spells repaid. Think about it.

Marshall McLuhan

The tiny madman in his padded cell.

Vladimir Nabokov

I can't think why mothers love them. All babies do is leak at both ends.

Douglas Feaver

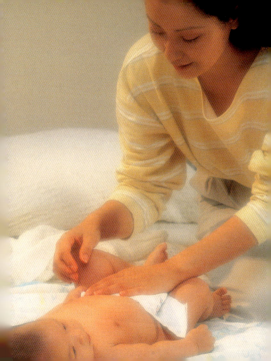

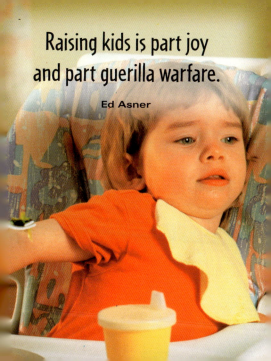

Getting down on
all fours
and imitating a
rhinoceros stops
babies
from crying.

P. J. O'Rourke

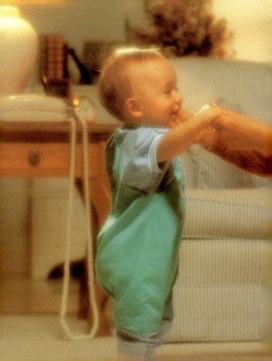

We spend the first twelve months of our children's lives teaching them to walk and talk and the next twelve telling them to sit down and shut up.

Phyllis Diller

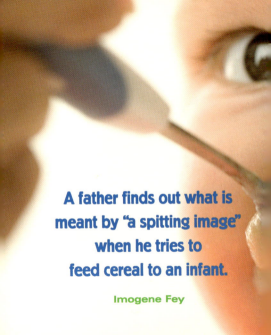

A three year old child
is a being who gets
almost as much fun
out of a fifty-six dollar
set of swings as
it does out of finding
a small green worm.

Bill Vaughan

Every child is born a genius.

Buckminster Fuller

In America there are two classes of travel—first class, and with children.

Robert Benchley

Since people are going to be living longer and getting older, they'll just have to learn how to be babies longer.

Andy Warhol

A perfect example
of minority rule
is a baby
in the house.

Milwaukee Journal

A baby is born with a need to be loved and never outgrows it.

Frank A. Clark

Photo Credits

Front jacket, pages 1, 3, & 14: © Coneyl Jay/Image Bank/Getty Images

Back jacket & page 19: © Ryan McVay/Photodisc Green/Getty Images

Page 7: © Donna Day/Photodisc Green/Getty Images

Page 8: © Photodisc Red/Getty Images

Page 10: © Elke Van de Velde/Photodisc Red/Getty Images

Pages 13, 20, 31, 34, 40-41, 42, 45, 48, 51, 52, 55, 59, 60-61, 64-65, 66-67, 71, 75, 79, 80: © CORBIS

Pages 16-17: © Digital Vision/Getty Images

Page 23: © Alistair Berg/Photodisc Red/Getty Images

Page 24: © Stockbyte Platinum/Getty Images

Pages 26-27: © Jose Luis Pelaez, Inc./Blend Images/Getty Images

Page 28: © Ryan McVay/Photodisc Red/Getty Images

Pages 32-33: © David De Lossy/Photodisc Green/Getty Images

Page 37: © Andersen Ross/Photodisc Red/Getty Images

Page 38: © Dan Dalton/Photodisc Red/Getty Images

Page 47: © Ryan McVay/Photodisc Red/Getty Images

Page 56: © Nancy R. Cohen/Photodisc Red/Getty Images

Page 63: © Cohen/Ostrow/Digital Vision/Getty Images

Page 68: © Steve Mason/Photodisc Green/Getty Images

Page 72: © David De Lossy/Photodisc Green/Getty Images

Page 76: © Inti St Clair/Photodisc Red/Getty Images